This book belongs to:

The stories you are about to read are grounded in real life, reflecting the triumphs and trials of individuals who dared to dream. While these narratives are rooted in truth, we've taken care to respect privacy and avoid overt promotion by altering certain trademarked terms in illustrations. Dive in and let these tales inspire you, as they have been inspired by the world around us. Enjoy this journey, where truth is often more fascinating than fiction.

# Table of Contents

“I’m living a dream I never want to wake up from.”

Cristiano Ronaldo

# The Humble Beginnings

## CHAPTER 1

Howdy, my name is Cristiano Ronaldo, but my close pals just call me Cris. I'm originally from a small but beautiful island named Madeira, part of the wonderful country of Portugal. Madeira is simply dazzling, graced with an endless embrace of the warm sun and bordered by an expansive sea of blue that stretches as far as the eye can see. It's as if the sea is trying to mirror the wide-open sky above.

Our family didn't have a lot of money when I was a kid. We didn't own fancy stuff or live in a big house. Instead, our humble home was packed with something more valuable: love and warmth. Sure, we didn't have a lot of material things, but we were rich in so many other ways. We were rich because we had each other's backs, supporting one another through thick and thin.

My mom, she's the real superhero of our family. She was always there, working tirelessly to make sure we never went to bed hungry. My dad was my first soccer coach, teaching me the basics of the game that would one day become my life. Then there were my siblings, who were my very first playmates and friends. They cheered me on, whether we were playing in our backyard or I was trying to perfect a new trick with my soccer ball.

Ever since I can remember, there was one thing that set my heart on fire: soccer. Whenever I was playing soccer, it felt as if the rest of the world just faded into the background. I could be anybody, I could be anywhere.

As a kid, the streets of Madeira became my playing field, and my worn-out soccer ball was my loyal companion. I imagined the stone walls surrounding the streets were the boundaries of a massive soccer stadium, packed with fans chanting my name.

Every single day, come rain or shine, my friends and I would gather in those streets, our makeshift soccer field. We used two rocks as goal posts and started our games. Soccer was more than just a game for us. It was our dream, our unwritten promise to the future we eagerly wanted to grasp.

The best part about those street soccer games was the freedom. There were no coaches, no rules, just the pure joy of playing. We learned from each other, and more importantly, we learned from our mistakes. We fell, we got up, and we played on. That's how I learned to never give up, to keep trying until the last whistle blows.

My journey from the streets of Madeira to the biggest stadiums in the world wasn't easy. It took a lot of hard work, a lot of practice, and a lot of sacrifice. But through it all, I kept my love for soccer. Because at the end of the day, no matter where I am, when I'm on the soccer field, I'm just Cris from Madeira, living out his dream.

"Talent without working hard is nothing."

Cristiano Ronaldo

# CHAPTER 2

Soccer and I, we've been inseparable since I was a tiny tot. Right from the start, it was more than just a game to me. It was my sanctuary, my joy, my dream. I remember how the soccer field at our local park turned into a second home, how every practice session felt like the grandest adventure.

In the early morning haze or under the dusky twilight, I was always there, chasing the ball with unquenchable passion. I was just eight years old, but my dedication ran deep.

There came a special day that year, one that still shimmers in my heart like a precious gem. Our little town was hosting a soccer tournament and my heart pounded with excitement. It wasn't the grandeur of a World Cup or a Premier League match, but for me, it felt every bit as thrilling. I remember slipping into my well-worn soccer shoes, the ones I'd lovingly polished until they shone under the sun. I remember the chatter of my teammates, a symphony of laughter and nerves that filled the crisp morning air.

As we plunged into the games, every minute was a mixture of adrenaline, teamwork, and fierce determination. We played with all our might, as if each game was our final. When we won the tournament, the rush of joy was like a tidal wave.

It was our moment of glory, a moment of sweet victory that tasted like the freshest summer lemonade. But the magic didn't end there. In the midst of our joy, a surprise awaited me.

I was named the best player of the tournament. I felt my heart leap into my throat. The cheers of my teammates, the proud smiles of my parents, everything seemed to blend into a beautiful blur. And then they handed me a golden whistle instead of a trophy. Yes, you heard right - a golden whistle! I remember the confusion that momentarily clouded my happiness. A whistle? For me?

But as the local coach explained, the golden whistle was a symbol. It was for the little boy who was always guiding his teammates, always encouraging them. The boy who wasn't just playing, but also leading. In their eyes, I was a pint-sized referee, making sure we all played our best and played together.

That golden whistle became my most prized possession. It was not just a memento from a memorable day, but a token of recognition for the leader in me. Each time I saw it, I felt a surge of determination. It was a symbol of a dream I held dearly - a dream to play soccer, to lead, and to make it big. It was a constant reminder of the day I realized that I wasn't just Cristiano Ronaldo, the boy who loved soccer. I was Cristiano Ronaldo, the boy who was going to chase his dream, come what may. That golden whistle, my friends, was the sound of my dreams taking flight. And I was ready to soar.

"Your love makes me strong. Your hate makes me unstoppable."

Cristiano Ronaldo

# Moving to the Mainland

## CHAPTER 3

Packing up your whole life into a suitcase when you're just twelve years old is quite a big deal. That's exactly what I had to do. Leaving behind the familiar lanes and warm faces of my little island, Madeira, I embraced the unknown by stepping foot in Lisbon.

This massive city was a world away from my humble hometown. The towering buildings seemed to kiss the sky, the streets stretched on like never-ending paths, and the constant buzz of city noise was a stark contrast to the tranquil sound of sea waves I was accustomed to. But amongst all the new experiences, there was one that filled me with an uncontainable excitement – joining Sporting Lisbon Soccer Academy, one of Portugal's prestigious soccer schools!

My move to Lisbon wasn't all about the excitement of the new environment. It was also a drastic change that was challenging. Instead of the cozy family home I was used to, I found myself in dorms at the academy, living amongst other young soccer enthusiasts like myself. Late at night, lying on my bed, I'd miss the comforting sounds of my home. The taste of my mom's delicious bacalhau, the rhythmic sound of my dad's voice as he narrated a story, the playful banter with my siblings, all seemed miles away. It was a lonely period, but I knew it was the price for my dreams.

The soccer field at the academy was a place of refuge, a home away from home. A lush, green oasis, it was bigger and more beautiful than any field I'd seen before. Every morning, tying up the laces of my cleats, I'd step onto this field, the nervousness replaced by a sense of belonging and passion. The feel of the ball against my foot, the encouraging cheers of my teammates, the exhilarating thrill of scoring a goal - all these things reminded me of why I was there.

While Lisbon gave me the opportunity to enhance my soccer skills, it also provided life's essential lessons. Falling and getting back up, persisting through the tough times, and realizing that the journey to success isn't always smooth, were all lessons learned on and off the field. The road to my dreams was filled with obstacles and challenges, but the love for soccer and belief in my dream fueled my strength and resilience.

Even in the face of hardships, I never stopped moving forward. The longing for home and the intense training schedule were tough, but the love for soccer and the dream I was chasing always gave me the motivation to continue. Because with each passing day in Lisbon, I was one step closer to turning my dream into reality.

Being in Lisbon taught me to trust the journey. It taught me that even if you're miles away from home, and even if the road is rocky, if you have a dream and the passion to achieve it, you can find the strength to keep going. And with that strength, and with that dream, I took one step at a time, moving closer to the dream that was driving me all along.

"I am not a perfectionist, but I like to feel that things are done well."

Cristiano Ronaldo

# The Magical Match Against Manchester

## CHAPTER 4

A few years zipped by and suddenly I was standing in the middle of a giant, buzzing stadium. It was a sizzling summer day in 2003, and we were playing a friendly match against Manchester United. Now, I wasn't playing for just any team — I was playing for Sporting Lisbon! This was a big deal. It wasn't just any other game, you see. We were opening our brand new stadium, and I was about to play the most important game of my life.

Even though I was 18, which sounds pretty grown up, I felt a million butterflies fluttering in my stomach. But deep down, I was ready. The moment I stepped onto the grass, I could hear the crowd. Oh, the crowd! It was like the sound of a roaring sea, waves of cheers and shouts that echoed around the stadium. I looked around and saw some of the biggest names in soccer. These were the players I admired, the players I aspired to be. And there I was, standing amongst them, ready to show them what I could do.

The whistle blew and the game began. I remember running like the wind, the ball at my feet like a faithful friend. I tackled harder than ever, my heart pounding in my chest. With every swoosh of the ball, every daring dribble, I gave it my all. I remember one moment where I sprinted towards the goal, my eyes focused, my mind clear. I took the shot... and scored! The crowd went wild, and in that moment, I felt like I was flying.

We won that game, and boy, did we celebrate! But the most incredible part wasn't just the win. It was what happened after. The manager of Manchester United, the legendary Sir Alex Ferguson, noticed how I played. Me, Cristiano Ronaldo, a boy from a small island, had caught the eye of one of the biggest soccer clubs in the world!

And just like that, my life was about to change. They wanted me, Cristiano, to play for them! I couldn't believe it. I was stepping into a dream, a dream so big it made my heart race. Little did I know, this was just the beginning of an incredible journey. A journey that would take me places I'd only dreamed of, a journey where I'd play not just good, but great, becoming one of the best soccer players the world has ever seen.

Not long after that game, I found myself in an airplane, flying across the sea towards a whole new adventure. Leaving Lisbon and Sporting Lisbon, the club that had been my home for several years, was bittersweet. But as the city lights started to fade away, I looked out the airplane window, with my heart filled with excitement and anticipation. Manchester United, one of the biggest soccer clubs in the world, was waiting for me.

Manchester was different from Lisbon in so many ways. It was bustling, with people always on the move. And the weather, oh, the weather! It was quite a switch from the sunny days I was used to back in Portugal. But the one thing that instantly made me feel at home was the love for soccer. Just like back in Madeira and Lisbon, soccer was the heartbeat of this city.

And as I pulled on the famous red jersey of Manchester United, marked with the number seven, I knew I had made it to yet another important milestone in my journey. I was ready to chase bigger dreams, ready to give my best, and ready to write a new chapter in my soccer story.

"I want to consistently play well and win titles. I'm only at the beginning."

Cristiano Ronaldo

# The Journey through Clubs

# CHAPTER 5

When you're a young player who dreams of becoming a professional, signing with a top club feels like an achievement. But it was only the beginning for me. At Manchester United, I transformed from a promising talent to a soccer star. I swapped my Sporting Lisbon jersey for Manchester United's famous red one. This shift was not just a change in colors; it was a stepping stone to higher challenges and larger victories.

My years at Manchester United were like attending a special school. I learned from the best in the field, including Sir Alex Ferguson, the legendary manager. I trained intensely, honed my skills, and developed a new understanding of the game. The club's rich history and culture humbled me, while their expectations fueled my ambition.

When I was just 23 years old, I achieved something incredible. I won the Ballon d'Or, awarded to the best soccer player in the world. I was no longer just a soccer player; I was a symbol of aspiration for many young players worldwide.

My journey continued, leading me to the glamorous Real Madrid. The sunny city of Madrid welcomed me with open arms and a white jersey. I became the most expensive player in the world, a title that filled me with both pride and responsibility. My years in Madrid were glittering, filled with personal achievements and club successes. We clinched La Liga and Champions League titles, and I added four more Ballon d'Or trophies to my collection.

Even after such colossal achievements, my thirst for new challenges didn't diminish. I moved to Juventus in Turin, Italy, and embraced a new culture, a new style of soccer. I learned to say "Ciao" and to appreciate a good plate of pasta. In Turin, I had the pleasure of adding more trophies to my cabinet, including two Serie A titles.

This journey through different clubs, countries, and cultures has been more than just about soccer. It has been a journey of personal growth, of understanding different people and learning new things. It has shaped me, not just as a player, but as a person, making me realize that soccer is more than a game. It's a lifestyle, a language that connects millions of hearts worldwide. And I feel fortunate to have lived this journey, every moment of it.

Then came another exciting chapter in my journey. I found myself back where it all really began: Manchester United. My return to Old Trafford, the place where I became a global star, felt like a homecoming. The fans welcomed me back with open arms and chants of "Viva Ronaldo!" echoing around the stadium. The thrill of pulling on the red jersey, feeling the familiar energy of the crowd, and scoring goals at the Stretford End... it was as if I'd never left.

So here I am, still playing the game I fell in love with on the streets of Madeira. Still chasing the ball, still pushing the limits, still living the dream. But the journey doesn't stop here. I still have more to learn, more to achieve, and more to give to this beautiful game. Because when you love what you do, age is just a number. My name is Cristiano Ronaldo, and this is my story so far. But trust me, there's more to come!

“I’ve never tried
to hide the fact that
it is my intention
to become the best.”

Cristiano Ronaldo

# The Number 7 Legacy

## CHAPTER 6

In the game of soccer, some numbers are more than just numbers. They are a sign of honor. They tell a story of great players who have come before. One such number is seven. When I joined Manchester United, I was given the number seven to wear on my jersey. It was a huge moment for me.

You see, at Manchester United, wearing the number seven is like wearing a superhero cape. Some of the best players in the world, like George Best, Bryan Robson, Eric Cantona, and David Beckham have all worn it. So, when the team manager, Sir Alex Ferguson, gave me a jersey with the number seven, it was like he was saying, "I believe in you." He thought I could be as good as the players who wore the number seven before me. That made me feel really special.

That's when the name CR7 was born. The 'CR' stands for my initials, Cristiano Ronaldo, and '7' is for my jersey number. It's a name that fans all over the world know me by now, not just on the soccer field, but off it too. It's even become a name for my own brand of clothing and perfumes!

Did you know the number seven is considered lucky in many places, including my home country, Portugal? Maybe it's been lucky for me too, because it pushed me to try harder, to be the best player I could be, just like the great number sevens before me.

Over time, the number seven has become a big part of who I am. It's not just a number on my jersey. It's a reminder of where I started, how much I've grown. It's part of my story, and that makes me proud. I'm not just Cristiano Ronaldo; I'm CR7.

Years passed, and the time came for me to leave Manchester United. I signed with Real Madrid, and I couldn't imagine wearing any other number but seven. But there was a small problem. The number seven jersey was already taken by a great player, Raul. However, Raul, with his kind heart, passed it to me when he left Real Madrid. Once again, I wore my superhero cape with pride, aiming to make history.

My years at Real Madrid were memorable. With the number seven on my back, I broke records and collected trophies. I became the first player in history to score 100 goals in European competition. I helped my team win two La Liga titles and four Champions League trophies. But most importantly, I continued the legacy of the number seven, further cementing its significance in the world of soccer.

Then came another shift, another move to a new team, Juventus. Again, the number seven was already taken, this time by Juan Cuadrado. But, similar to Raul, Juan graciously offered it to me. This gesture showed me once more the respect and unity in the soccer world. The number seven was once again mine, and I wore it with the same dedication and passion as I did at Manchester United and Real Madrid.

Looking back now, I realize that the number seven is not just a number for me. It represents a journey, a responsibility, and a promise. A journey from a young boy in Madeira to one of the best soccer players in the world. A responsibility to honor the legacy of the great players who wore it before me. And a promise to always give my best, to never stop chasing my dreams. Because at the end of the day, it's not about the number you wear, it's about what you do with it. And I am proud to say, I am CR7.

"Every season is a new challenge to me, and I always set out to improve in terms of games, goals, assists."

Cristiano Ronaldo

# The Euro Triumph

# CHAPTER 7

Ever tried to explain a rainbow to someone who's never seen one? That's how I feel when I think about leading Portugal to win the 2016 European Championship. This big event happens every four years. Think about it as a giant soccer party where the best teams from all the countries in Europe come to play. It's like the World Cup, but only for Europe. Being the captain, the leader of my team, during this amazing time was like living a dream.

At the start, things were a bit wobbly. We tied three times during the first set of games. It felt like we were trying to climb a huge mountain, but we couldn't see where we were going. Even with the tough start, we kept our heads up. We knew we could do something great. Every game, every minute of extra time, every penalty kick, made us a stronger team.

The quarter finals against Poland was like being on a roller coaster. The pressure was so heavy, we could almost touch it. But we didn't let that scare us. We held our breath, gave everything we had, and won the game during penalty kicks. Next, we had to play Wales in the semi-finals. We stood tall and scored two goals, getting us even closer to our dream.

The final game was against France. The energy was so high, I felt like I could touch the sky. But then, I got hurt early in the game and had to watch from the side. I felt so sad not being able to play, but I knew I was still part of the game. I cheered for my team, gave advice, and encouraged everyone from the sidelines.

During the extra time, our friend Eder scored the goal we'd been dreaming of. I felt a rush of happiness and relief. We did it! We were the champions of Europe! This wasn't just about winning a shiny trophy. It was about making a dream come true for us and for all the people in Portugal.

That special night taught me something really important. It doesn't matter how hard things seem or how many obstacles stand in your way. Never stop believing in yourself or your team. Winning isn't just for the fastest or the strongest, but for those who never give up, no matter how tough things get.

The moment the final whistle blew, I felt a wave of emotions. I looked at my teammates, their faces flushed with joy and disbelief. I looked at the trophy, glistening under the stadium lights, waiting to be lifted. I looked at the sea of fans, their cheers deafening. And then, I looked up at the sky, and I knew this moment would be etched in my heart forever. We, a small nation from the edge of Europe, had made history. We had proved that, with determination and unity, even the smallest can stand tall against the mightiest.

As I walked to the podium to lift the trophy, my heart pounded with pride. I lifted it high, the weight of it nothing compared to the joy in my heart.

"I don't have to show anything to anyone. There is nothing to prove."

Cristiano Ronaldo

# The Dream of Acting

## CHAPTER 8

As you may know, soccer has been my passion since I was a little boy. But it's not the only dream I've ever had. There's another one, a bit unusual, you might say – I've always been fascinated by the magic of movies and dreamed of becoming an actor one day.

Picture this – a big, fancy theater with comfy seats, popcorn smells wafting in the air, and a gigantic screen showcasing stories from far-off lands. Movies have always been a special kind of magic for me. They have the power to whisk you away to different worlds, make you laugh, make you cry, and most importantly, teach you important life lessons.

Ever since I was young, I wondered what it would be like to be on the other side of that big screen – to tell stories, to make people feel emotions, and to be a part of that magic. I thought it would be fun to try on different characters, just like how I try on different strategies in soccer.

So, after much thought, I decided to give it a shot. I took acting classes, practiced in front of the mirror, and even worked with a coach. I wanted to understand the craft and respect it, just like I did with soccer. I knew it wasn't going to be easy, but then again, nothing worth achieving ever is.

In 2019, I made my acting debut in a TV show. To say I was nervous would be an understatement. But I was also incredibly excited. I felt like a kid who had just been handed the golden ticket to Willy Wonka's chocolate factory. The experience was challenging, thrilling, and humbling, all at once.

Now, I'm not saying I'm going to win an Oscar or anything – although, you never know! What's important is that I followed my dream. I took a chance and tried something new. And in the end, that's what life's all about, isn't it? Chasing dreams, taking chances, and making the most of every opportunity.

So, who knows? Maybe one day you'll see me on the big screen. And if that day comes, I hope you'll be in the audience, cheering me on. Just remember — whether I'm on the soccer field or on the silver screen, I'm still the same Cristiano Ronaldo who once dreamed of big things back in Madeira. Dreams really can come true, my friends. And you know what? They're definitely worth chasing.

"I think sometimes the best training is to rest."

Cristiano Ronaldo

# CHAPTER 9

Being known worldwide for my soccer skills is a gift, but what I value even more is the chance to make a difference in people's lives. Throughout my successful career, I've always strived to be mindful of the struggles that others face, far from the glamour and excitement of the soccer field.

One way I've found to help is by donating blood regularly. It's a simple act, but it has the potential to save lives. For this reason, I've chosen not to get a tattoo, which would prevent me from donating blood as often as I do.

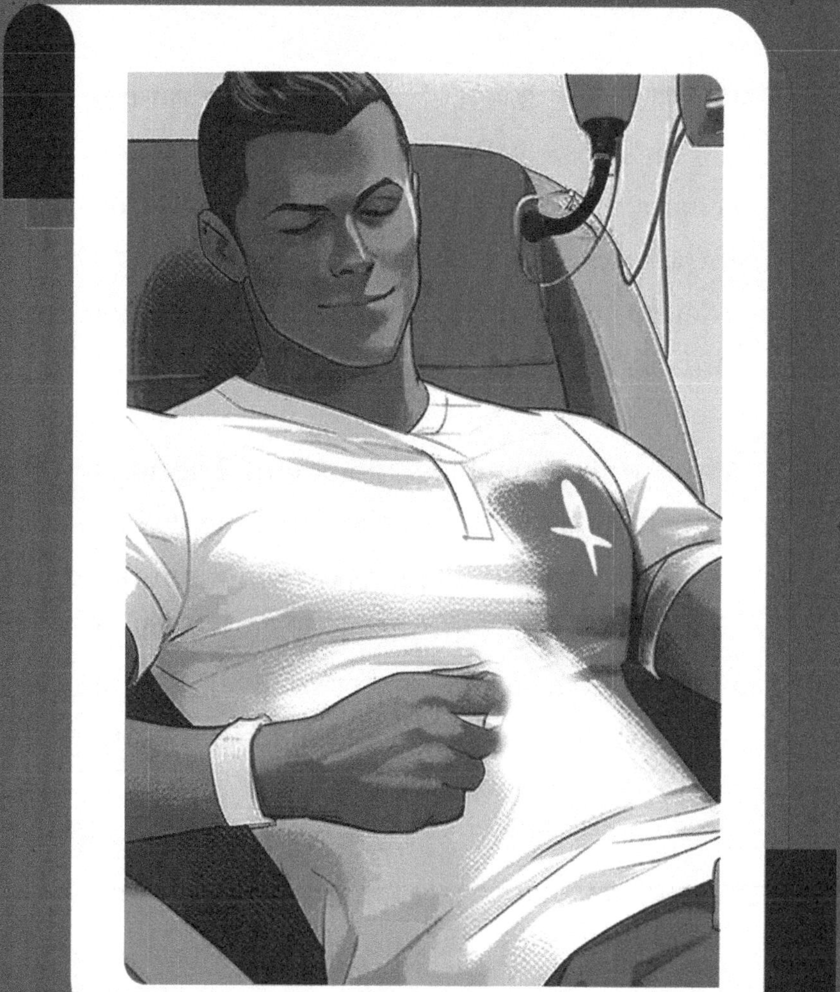

This decision has had a deep impact on my life. For instance, I was able to help a young boy named Erik Ortiz Cruz, who was suffering from a severe brain disorder. His family was burdened with medical bills they couldn't afford, and Erik needed surgery.

Along with regular blood donations, I decided to step in and cover his medical treatment. The joy on Erik's face when he recovered was more rewarding than any trophy I've ever won. It was a testament to the power of small acts of kindness, and a reminder of why I choose to live my life the way I do.

In another touching instance, I was privileged to meet a brave little girl from Kyrgyzstan named Yuna. She was battling a tough illness and was in an Italian hospital for treatment. Despite the language barrier, her spirit and resilience were awe-inspiring. Meeting Yuna reminded me of the immense strength and courage that people, including children, can show in the face of adversity.

But my efforts aren't just limited to individuals. I've made substantial donations to numerous charitable causes, such as children's hospitals and cancer centers. It's not simply about signing a check; it's about spreading hope and kindness. After all, when you're in a position to make a difference, why wouldn't you?

Soccer has given me the world, and I believe in giving back to the world too. It's not just about the donations and individual acts of kindness. I have used my influence to shed light on issues that matter.

To me, philanthropy is a journey as exciting and meaningful as my soccer career. It's a journey of understanding, empathy, and sharing. It's about making a difference in the lives of others, making them smile, and giving them hope. It's about being a good human being and setting an example for the younger generation. I want to show them that success is not just about scoring goals, but also about using that success to score goals for humanity. Because, in the end, we are all part of the same team - Team Humanity.

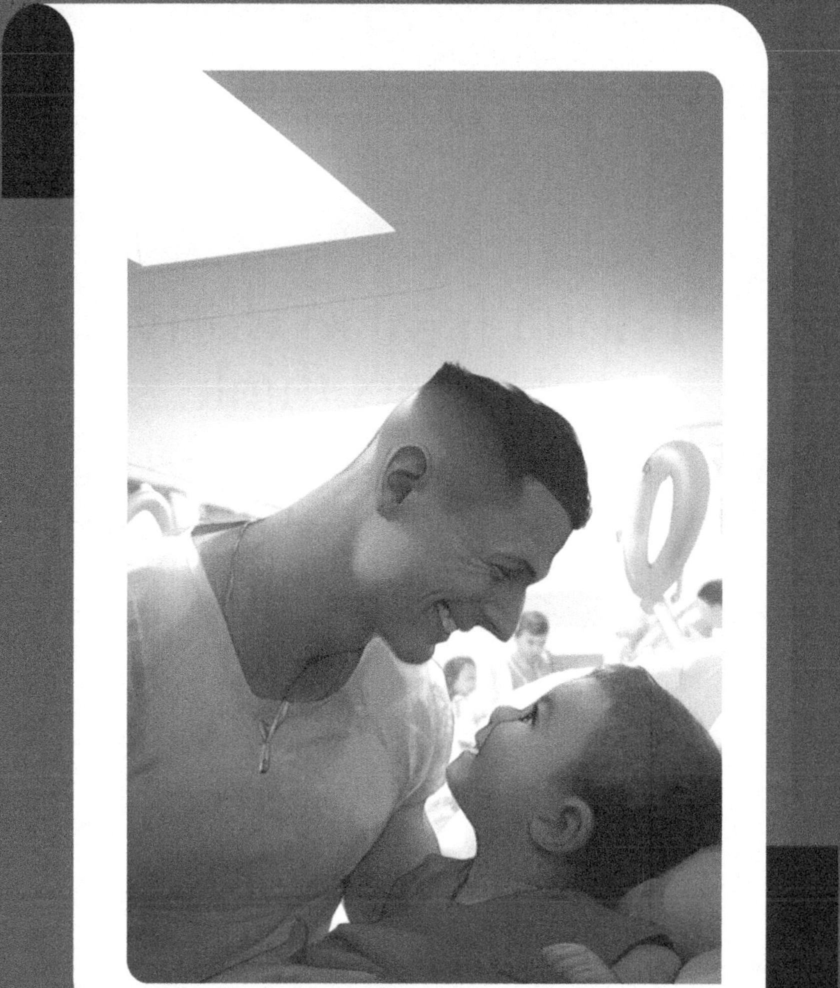

“I don’t have to worry
what others think
I talk when I want to.
Everybody knows who I am,
what I believe in.”

Cristiano Ronaldo

# The Taste of Defeat

## CHAPTER 10

Soccer is like a roller coaster, full of thrilling ups and stomach-dropping downs. There are times when we jump for joy, and times when we hang our heads low. And the truth is, no one—not even me, Cristiano Ronaldo—can win all the time. Losing is a part of the ride, and although it might not be the fun part, it's still a part that matters.

To me, every time we lose, it's like life is giving us a pop quiz. It's a chance to stop, think, and try to figure out what didn't quite work. Even on days when I give my best and things don't go as planned, these are the moments that really test who I am – kind of like standing at a fork in the road: one way is feeling sorry for ourselves, and the other is using the setback as a springboard to bounce back even higher.

I can't forget one particular loss. It was in the 2004 European Championship final, right in my home country of Portugal. The excitement in the air was electric, and the fans were cheering us on like crazy.

The championship felt so close, I could almost reach out and touch it. But the game didn't go our way, and we ended up in second place. That loss left a sour taste in my mouth – like watching an ice cream cone slip from your hand just as you're about to take a bite.

But here's the cool part about dreams – they're tougher than any loss. Sure, we lost that game, and sure, it was a bummer. But that loss didn't put out the fire inside me. In fact, it stoked the flames. It made me want to fight for victory even harder. That sour taste of losing turned into a hunger to get better, to work harder, and to never let the fear of a loss keep me from giving my all.

So yes, losing can be a real drag. It can make your heart feel heavy and leave a yucky feeling in your gut. But if you take a moment to learn from it, it can lead to something really amazing – it can clear the way for a comeback that's even sweeter than the victory you were hoping for. That's the magic of soccer. That's the magic of life.

The End

Dear Wonderful Parents and Kids,

We hope you enjoyed our book! If you could take a moment to leave a rating for us on Amazon, it would greatly help us. Your feedback not only supports our work but also helps other readers. Thank you!

Made in the USA
Las Vegas, NV
03 December 2023

82013862R00049